A class visit to the great Mohammed Ali Mosque in Cairo.

A father shows his daughter one of her country's pyramids.

A family picnic outside the mosque.

The farm day starts for a sister and two brothers.

Waiting for tourists in front of the great sphinx and pyramid.

ROTHERHAM LIBRARY AND INFORMATION SERVICES

This book must be returned by the date specified at the time of issue as
the DATE DUE for RETURN.

The loan may be extended (personally, by post or telephone) for a
further period, if the book is not required by another reader, by quoting
the above number/author/title.

LIS 7a

Meeting with friends in the market cafe.

A village school principal (right) with one of the school's teachers.

Three owners of a Luxor restaurant.

A gigantic Pharaoh's statue is all that remains of his ancient temple.

A tour guide tells tourists about the amazing lives of the Pharaohs and their gods.

EGYPT
the people

Arlene Moscovitch

A Bobbie Kalman Book

The Lands, Peoples, and Cultures Series

 Crabtree Publishing Company

The Lands, Peoples, and Cultures Series

Created by Bobbie Kalman

Coordinating editor
Ellen Rodger

Project development
First Folio Resource Group, Inc.
  Pauline Beggs
  Tom Dart
  Kathryn Lane
  Debbie Smith

Editing
Joyce Funamoto

Photo research
Robyn Craig

Design
David Vereschagin/Quadrat Communications

Separations and film
Dot 'n Line Image Inc.

Printer
Worzalla Publishing Company

Special thanks to
Sally Abuseif, Heather Dalgleish,
Prof. Dr. Ahmed ElSherbini, Consul, Bureau
of Cultural and Education Affairs of Egypt;
Dr. N. B. Millet, Senior Curator, Egyptian
Section, Royal Ontario Museum; Magda
Mousa, Principal, MISR Language School,
André L. Potvin, Ms. Elham Yassin

Photographs
Archive/Photo Researchers: p. 7 (top left);
Corbis/Bettmann: p. 9 (bottom);
Corbis/Bettmann-UPI: p. 9 (top); Corbis/Marc Garanger: p.
22 (bottom); Marc Crabtree: cover, title page, front endpaper
page 1 (top left, bottom right), page 2 (bottom left), rear
endpaper page 1 (top left, middle, bottom left), rear endpaper
page 2 (top, middle left and right); p. 4 (both), p. 5 (bottom),
p. 10 (left), p. 11 (top), pp. 12–14 (all), p. 15 (bottom), p. 19
(bottom), p. 21 (left), pp. 25–28 (all), p. 29 (top and bottom
left), p. 31 (bottom); Peter Crabtree: front endpaper page 1
(top right, middle, bottom left), page 2 (top left, right, middle
bottom left), rear endpaper page 1 (top left, bottom left), rear
endpaper page 2 (bottom), p. 7 (right), p. 23 (top); Louise
Goldman/Photo Researchers: p. 15 (top); Sylvain
Grandadam/Photo Researchers: p. 18; Imapress/Archive
Photos: p. 11 (bottom); Guy W. Midkiff: p. 20; Richard T.
Nowitz: p. 6 (bottom), p. 8 (both), p. 10 (right), p. 16, p. 17
(middle), p. 21 (right), p. 22 (top), p. 23 (bottom), p. 24 (both),
p. 30 (both); C. Osborne /Photo Researchers: p. 31 (top); Carl
Purcell: p. 15 (middle); Reuters/Aladin Abdel-nabi/Archive
Photos: p. 19 (top); Scala/Art Resource, NY: p. 6 (top);
SEF/Art Resource, NY: p. 3; Werner Forman/Art Resource,
NY: p. 7 (bottom left); Laura Zito/Photo Researchers:
p. 17 (top and bottom), p. 29 (bottom right)
Every effort has been made to obtain the appropriate credit and full copyright
clearance for all images in this book. Any oversites, despite Crabtree's
greatest precautions, will be corrected in future editions.

Illustrations
William Kimber. Male and female hieroglyphs appear at the
head of each section. The Great Sphinx is shown on the back
cover.

Cover: A young woman wears a headscarf to shade herself
from the hot Egyptian sun.

Title page: Two Egyptians return from market with their
newly purchased sheep.

Published by
Crabtree Publishing Company

PMB 16A,350 Fifth Ave.	360 York Road, RR 4,	73 Lime Walk
Suite 3308	Niagara-on-the-Lake,	Headington
New York	Ontario, Canada	Oxford OX3 7AD
N.Y. 10118	L0S 1J0	United Kingdom

Cataloging in Publication Data
Moscovitch, Arlene, 1946-
    Egypt, the people / Arlene Moscovitch.
      p. cm. -- (The lands, peoples, and cultures series)
    Includes index.
    4-9.
      Summary: Describes the lives of people in modern Egypt--
with mention of ancient times--discussing life in villages, in
cities, and in the desert, festivals, family events, clothing,
foods, and more.
      ISBN 0-86505-233-6 (RLB). -- ISBN 0-86505-313-8 (paper)
      1. Egypt--Social life and customs Juvenile literature.
[1.Egypt--Social life and customs.] I. Title. II. Series.
DT107.826.M67 2000
962--dc21
                                                    LC 99-16638
                                                          CIP

Contents

4   Modern people, ancient past

6   A trip through history

10   The people

12   Village life

14   City life

16   Desert life

18   Islam

20   Festivals

22   Family events

24   Sports and pastimes

26   School days

28   Clothes

30   Food

32   Glossary and Index

Modern people, ancient past

Today's Egyptians live in a land that has the longest recorded history of any country in the world. Their way of life, religion, clothing, homes, and food have all been influenced by the many different peoples who have lived in Egypt over thousands of years and by the geography of the country.

Even today, people in many parts of Egypt lead lives that are very similar to the lives of people thousands of years ago. Some farmers till the rich soil by the Nile River as their **ancestors** did in ancient Egypt. Other Egyptians lead a more modern lifestyle in bustling cities like Alexandria and Cairo. Some people roam the arid desert while others cluster around its **fertile**, green **oases**. Wherever they live, Egypt's people are never far from the magnificent **monuments** that remind them of their country's glorious past.

Egyptian youngsters often help their parents.
This girl tends her parents' vegetable stand.

A young Egyptian.

High school students eagerly pose for their graduation photo with their principal and guests.

A smiling woman is shielded from the hot Egyptian sun by layers of loose clothing.

5

Egypt's statues, **temples,** and **tombs** are reminders of the country's long and rich history. For over 5000 years, Egypt has lived through many changes. Now an independent nation, Egypt has been both a powerful **empire**, and a **colony**.

Land of the Pharaohs

People have lived in the land of Egypt for thousands of years. Before 3100 B.C., Egypt was divided into Upper Egypt and Lower Egypt. In 3100 B.C., these two lands were united into a single kingdom, ruled by a king, or **Pharaoh**. The **reign** of the Pharaohs of ancient Egypt lasted for almost 3000 years. Through all those centuries, a great **civilization** grew up on the banks of the Nile River. The ancient Egyptians built magnificent monuments. They made pottery, beautiful gold and silver jewelry, and furniture. They created their own symbols for writing and kept written records. They **worshiped** many gods and believed in a life after death.

Hatshepsut
1478 B.C.–1458 B.C.
Hatshepsut was a powerful Pharaoh who sent troops into battle, sent traders out to the seas, and built beautiful temples. One thing makes this ruler very different from ancient Egypt's other Pharaohs – Hatshepsut was a woman! In the paintings and carvings on temples and tombs, she wears men's clothes, including the royal ceremonial beard. Despite her clothing, most Egyptians knew that they were being led by a woman: Hatshepsut means "foremost of the noble women."

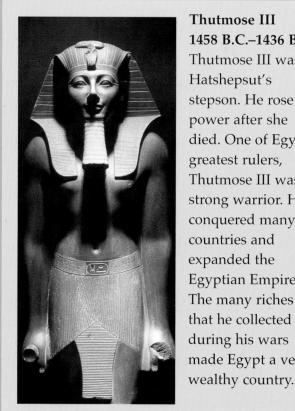

Thutmose III
1458 B.C.–1436 B.C.
Thutmose III was Hatshepsut's stepson. He rose to power after she died. One of Egypt's greatest rulers, Thutmose III was a strong warrior. He conquered many countries and expanded the Egyptian Empire. The many riches that he collected during his wars made Egypt a very wealthy country.

Ruled by foreigners

By 1000 B.C., the rule of the Pharaohs was in decline. Over most of the next 3000 years, non-Egyptians ruled Egypt. These rulers came from many places, including Libya, Greece, Rome, Arabia, Turkey, France, and England. In 332 B.C., the Greek emperor Alexander the Great **conquered** Egypt. He founded the city of Alexandria, which became a major center of Greek learning and culture. The last of the Greek rulers, Queen Cleopatra, died in 30 B.C. For more than 500 years after her death, Egypt was a province of the Roman Empire, a territory that covered the Mediterranean region and beyond.

Akhenaton (Amenhotep IV)
1367 B.C.–1350 B.C.
Akhenaton was a rebel. He tried to change the religion of Egypt from the worship of many gods to the worship of one god. Many people did not agree with his beliefs. After Akhenaton's death, the rulers of Egypt turned back to the old religion and tried their best to erase all traces of his unpopular rule.

Ramses II
1290 B.C.–1224 B.C.
Ramses II would love his modern nickname – Ramses the Great. He was a clever politician who conquered many lands, but also made peace with his enemies. He built huge temples all over Egypt, including many to honor himself. To the Egyptians he must have seemed a god. So many years ago, people were lucky if they lived until they were 40 years old. Ramses ruled until his death, at the age of 92 years!

Cleopatra is one of the most famous women in history. A strong ruler, she was known for her charm and ambition.

The Arabs arrive

In 639 A.D., the Arabs invaded and Egypt became part of the great Arab Empire, which stretched from Spain to India. Most Egyptians adopted Islam, the religion of their rulers. They also began speaking Arabic, their rulers' language, instead of the ancient Egyptian language and Greek. Power struggles continued in Egypt. Starting in 1250, Egypt was ruled by the Mamluks for 300 years. The Mamluk rulers were slaves who rose through the ranks of the Egyptian armies. Then, in 1517, the Turks invaded Egypt and made the country part of their empire until 1919.

During their rule, the Mamluks built many beautiful mosques, Islamic places of worship.

(top) The Arab ruler Ahmed Ibn Tulun had this mosque built in 879. It is the oldest mosque in Cairo.

In 1919, a woman makes a speech at a political rally protesting the British presence in Egypt.

From colony to kingdom

Even though Egypt was part of the Turkish Empire in the early 1900s, British power and influence grew in the country. At that time, many **colonies** and countries around the world were under the rule of the British Empire. During World War I (1914–1918), Britain declared Egypt a protected country under British rule and drove the Turks out. In 1922, Britain granted Egypt independence. King Fuad became the ruler of Egypt. However, the real power in the country was not with the king, but with the British Empire. After King Fuad died in 1936, his son Farouk became the next king of Egypt.

Independence at last

In 1952, the Egyptians forced the British out of Egypt. Army officers took over power and forced the unpopular King Farouk to leave the country. For the first time in almost 20 centuries, Egypt was ruled completely by Egyptians. The country became the Arab Republic of Egypt, with both a president and a prime minister leading the country.

Gamal Abdel Nasser helped lead the revolt against King Farouk. This popular leader was the president of Egypt from 1956 until his death in 1970.

The people

Modern Egyptians are a mixture of all the peoples who settled in Egypt during the past 5000 years. They include people from Africa, Asia, the Middle East, and Europe, as well as the ancient Egyptians. Today, about half of Egypt's people live in cities. The other half live in farming villages, oases, and the desert.

Egyptian Arabs

Like the Arabs who invaded Egypt 1400 years ago, most Egyptians today speak Arabic and follow the religion of Islam. Followers of Islam are called Muslims. They worship *Allah,* the Arabic word for God, and follow the teachings of his **prophet** Muhammad. The remaining Egyptians are mainly Christians called **Copts**. They follow the teachings of Jesus Christ, who they believe was God's son on earth.

Bedouins

For thousands of years, Bedouin tribes have traveled the deserts with their camels and goats. They are **nomads**, always searching for grazing land for their animals and fresh water for their families. They travel in large family groups. The leader of a group is called the *sheik*. Bedouins carry their homes with them wherever they go. They live in tents of goat and camel hair, which the women weave on their **looms**. Bedouins are known for their **hospitality**. Visitors are always invited to stay for three days and three nights, and to share stories with their hosts. Life is changing for the Bedouin. Many of them now live in houses and use trucks for transportation instead of camels.

(above) This young girl lives in Cairo, Egypt's capital city.

(right) A young Bedouin waits patiently with his dog and camel.

*A Nubian family relaxes
in their living room.*

*In a tent on the Siwa Oasis, boys
listen to friends playing music.*

Nubians

Nubians have lived in southern Egypt since the time of the Pharaohs. They worked for the Pharaohs as highly trained soldiers and as traders, carrying goods on their boats to and from other countries. They also used their boats to haul rock, and to transport villagers along the Nile River. Nubians used to farm the narrow strip of fertile land along the Nile. When the first **dam** was built at Aswan in 1902, its rising waters forced the Nubian people to move from the edge of the river to higher ground. This earth was **barren** and it was very difficult to grow crops. Many Nubian men had to go to the cities to find work. In the 1960s, there was more flooding when the Aswan High Dam was built. The Nubians were given more fertile land farther north, which allowed many of the men to stay with their families and work the land.

The Siwan people

The Siwan people live in the Siwa Oasis in the Western Desert. There, underground springs of water make it possible for people to grow crops, such as olives and dates. Like most Egyptians, the Siwan are Muslims, but they speak the Siwan language, not Arabic. They have their own special customs. One Siwan tradition is that on the evening before her wedding, the bride-to-be is led to a pool of water outside her village. There, an older woman bathes her. On the way home, the family of her husband-to-be meets her and gives her many gifts. Among these gifts are 40 dresses. She must wear seven of these, one on top of the other, on her wedding day.

11

 # Village life

In ancient times, Egyptian farmers did much of the work in the country. They helped build the Pharaoh's tombs and monuments. They also grew the food that fed the other workers. Today, most farmers, or *fellahin*, live where their ancestors did, in small villages along the Nile River.

Village homes

Newer villages have wide streets and houses that are made of sand bricks or cement blocks made in factories. In older villages, narrow streets are filled with people and animals, and the houses are close together. Many of the houses are built of bricks made from the Nile's mud. Villagers lay the bricks in rows where the hot sun bakes them. When the bricks are dry and hard, all the people in a family build their own house. Sometimes, they trim the walls in blue because they believe that this color protects them from bad luck.

Often, houses have a shady courtyard in the middle. The refreshing air here cools down the rooms that surround the courtyard. Families relax in the courtyard and may also prepare their meals here instead of in the hot, stuffy kitchen.

Farming

Only seven percent of Egypt's land is good for growing crops. The rest of the country is desert. On their plots of fertile land, *fellahin* plant beans, wheat, corn, and date palm trees. They also raise goats, ducks, and pigeons for their meat, and water buffalo for their milk. The water buffalo also plow the fields and work pumps that water the land. There are more people in Egypt than there used to be and there is less land for farming. Today, many people who live in villages work in cities or nearby towns. Some Egyptians even go to other countries to work.

(opposite) Most village houses have flat roofs, which Egyptians use as open-air bedrooms during the hottest times of the year.

Women do the laundry together in the village street.

Everyday chores

Everyone in a *fellahin* family has a job to do. The men till the fields or work in factories and shops in towns or cities. The women prepare the food, look after the house and the children, and care for the animals. Some husbands and wives work together in small family businesses. *Fellahin* children usually do their chores in the afternoon, when school is finished for the day. Young children help by herding the sheep and goats. Boys learn how to farm the land. Girls fetch water, milk the goats and water buffalo, and feed the chickens. When they are young, girls learn to carry loads on their heads. They start with loaves of bread. Then, after a lot of practice, they can walk and balance large clay jars of water on their heads without spilling a single drop!

Family and friends

In an Egyptian village, people never have to worry about being alone. Uncles, aunts, cousins, and grandparents are always there to keep someone company or lend a helping hand. Often, the whole family works together and family members look after each other. If one person's crops are damaged, all the relatives share what they have. If an animal is badly injured and has to be killed, family members buy some of the meat. This way, *fellahin* have enough money to buy another animal.

A girl tends a baby goat.

A farmer harvests his crops by hand.

Egyptian cities are a mix of the old and the new, a place where the worlds of Africa, Europe, and Asia meet. These days, more Egyptians live in cities than ever before, especially in the busy cities of Alexandria and Cairo. Many people from the countryside have moved here, looking for work and a place to live. Cairo, the **capital**, grows by the day and its suburbs now stretch into the desert.

City homes

There is so little wood in Egypt that most city buildings are made of brick or cement, which are plentiful. The kinds of buildings vary, depending on the neighborhood. New neighborhoods have large houses or modern apartment buildings. In the older parts of town, large families squeeze into tiny apartments with balconies that overhang the twisting, narrow streets. As more people crowd into the cities, it becomes harder to find a place to live.

Small apartment buildings crowd this Cairo neighborhood.

Tons of traffic

In Egyptian cities, the traffic never stops. Cars, buses, trucks, donkey carts, and crowds of people spill over the roads in every direction. Horns blare and loud music from thousands of radios fills the air. The cities are very crowded and it can take quite a long time to travel from one place to another, especially during rush hour. If you want to get a spot on a crowded bus, be prepared to shove your way aboard!

Different neighborhoods

Egyptian cities are an exciting blend of neighborhoods and people. Some people follow ancient traditions and others lead modern lifestyles. Some people are rich and others are poor. Often, these people live side by side. Beautiful homes are built beside modest shacks. Lawyers, doctors, professors, and business people on their way to work pass families picking through garbage, looking for something to sell. **Shantytowns**, where people live in small huts, lie on the outskirts of cities. Nearby, air conditioners hum and satellite dishes speckle the roofs of modern houses and apartment buildings.

Cars jam the streets at a main intersection in Cairo.

(below) People shop in the clothing section of a market.

(above) After hanging the wash, a woman watches the busy streets below.

Trying to narrow the gap

In Egypt, the gap between the rich and the poor seems to grow greater each year. Those people who could afford to go to school when they were younger learned how to read and write. Many of them have good jobs. Other people who had to work when they were younger never learned to read or write. Now, many of these people are poor and unemployed. The government is working hard to change the situation and to make sure that everyone has access to a good education, health care, and nutritious food.

15

*A Bedouin family makes its way through
the Sinai Desert to the next camp site.*

Some desert dwellers, like the Siwan people, live in towns and villages built on oases. Others, like the Bedouin, are nomadic. They do not stay in one spot for very long. Wherever they go in the desert, they take their families, their animals, and their houses with them.

Reading the desert

In the Arabic language, Bedouin means "people of the desert." After thousands of years of moving all over the desert, the Bedouin know how to read the clues the desert leaves for them. Without this knowledge, they would not be able to survive in such a harsh land. When they see tracks in the sand, they know that travelers passed that way before, from which direction they came, what kinds of animals they had with them, and even the age of their camels. Shrubs and plants tell them when it last rained and how much rain fell. Even though the desert might look the same in almost every direction, Bedouins do not get lost. They navigate the seas of sand by the stars, by markers they left behind on other trips, and by familiar landmarks.

Desert homes

The traditional Bedouin home is a movable wool tent. The tent is divided in two by a woven curtain called a *ma'nad.* One part is called the *mag'ad,* or sitting place. This is where the men and most guests sit. The other part is the *maharama,* or place of the women. When the tribe moves, Bedouin women take down their family's home. They pack it on the camel's back and then put it up again in their new location. When it is very hot, Bedouins roll up the tent flaps so air can enter. In a sandstorm, the flaps are pinned down to keep the tent from blowing over. If a Bedouin husband and wife divorce, the woman keeps the tent. The man keeps the goats and camels.

Bedouins camp at the foot of mountain cliffs.

Changing times

Life in the desert is slowly becoming more modern. Some Bedouins were given land by the government and now live in houses rather than tents. Instead of searching for water with their camels, they receive it by truck in 450-liter (100-gallon) barrels. Cars can now reach parts of the desert where only the Bedouin and their camels could travel before. Today, many Bedouins stand at the crossroads between two different worlds. The old ways are slowly changing, and the Bedouin are not quite sure what the future will bring.

(above) Bedouin men chat as they wait for a pot of coffee to brew.

A young Bedouin pulls water from a well to quench her camels' thirst.

Islam

More than 90 percent of all Egyptians are Muslims. There are two main groups of Muslims: the Sunni and the Shi'ites. Both groups use the same *Qur'an*, follow Muhammad's teachings, and share many of the same beliefs. There is one big difference, though. When Muhammad died, some of his followers thought that they should vote for the next leader. The people who followed this leader became Sunni Muslims. Other followers thought that the next leader should be a member of Muhammad's family, and chose his son-in-law, Ali. These were Shi'ite Muslims. Most Muslims in Egypt are Sunni.

Muslim girls study the **Qur'an.**

The lunar year
The Islamic year is based on the phases of the moon. It is about eleven days shorter than the solar year of 365 days. According to the solar calendar, holidays such as Ramadan shift about eleven days back each year. One year, the month of Ramadan may occur in the summer. Ten years later, Ramadan may be in the middle of winter!

A way of life
For many Muslims, Islam is more than a religion. It is also a way of life. Muslims read *Allah's* words in the *Qu'ran*, the **holy** book of Islam. The *Qur'an* lays out many basic rules, such as what to eat and drink. Muslims also read about Muhammad's sayings and deeds in *hadith.* Each *hadith* is a story about Muhammad that shows how wise he was and what a good life he led. By trying to follow Muhammad's example, Muslims believe they will come closer to leading a peaceful and meaningful life.

The Five Pillars of Islam
There are five things that all religious Muslims must try to do. First, they must declare their **faith** in front of other people. Second, they must pray to *Allah* five times every day: at daybreak, noon, afternoon, sunset, and evening. Every year, they must give a certain amount of money to people in need. They must **fast** from dawn to sunset every day during the holy month of Ramadan. Finally, those who can, make a **pilgrimage** to Mecca, the holy city in the country of Saudi Arabia where Muhammad was born. This pilgrimage is called a *hajj.*

Ramadan
Ramadan is the ninth and holiest month of the Islamic year. During Ramadan, religious Muslims do not eat or drink anything from sunrise to sunset. Children up to the age of twelve and pregnant women do not usually fast. Muslims believe fasting teaches them **self-discipline** and reminds them of all the good things that *Allah* has given them. When the sun goes down, people break their fast with a few dates or a glass of water. Then, they eat a big meal called *iftar.* After *iftar,* large crowds jam the streets to listen to storytellers and musicians. Stores and restaurants stay open late, and people visit family and friends.

Eid al-Fitr

Ramadan ends with a joyful celebration called Eid al-Fitr. Eid lasts for three days and is a public holiday. Traditionally, everyone gets new clothes. Houses are filled with flowers and are often decorated with banners. Children, especially, look forward to Eid because they receive toys, candy, and new clothing. Often, every door in the neighborhood is open and families stop by with gifts to share a midday feast together.

So many people have come to the mosque, a Muslim place of worship, that a whole crowd must pray outside.

Muslim men wait to eat during Ramadan. As soon as the sun sets, the fast will be over for the day.

Festivals

The Egyptian year is crammed with festivals. Some celebrate the ancient **heritage** of the land, others celebrate the religion of the people who live there, and still others celebrate important people and special times of the year.

Moulids

Moulids, or festivals of religious figures, are huge, popular gatherings that Muslims and Christians look forward to every year. Each town, village, and city has its own *moulid.* A *moulid* may last from two days to two weeks. People crowd into the streets to listen to musicians and storytellers, and to watch the religious dancers known as **dervishes**. Adults visit each other, while children enjoy fun-filled carnivals with all kinds of rides and games.

People watch dazzling displays of lights or take part in long, winding parades. The most impressive parade takes place in Cairo for the Moulid el-Nabi. This festival honors the birthday of the Muslim prophet Muhammad.

Sham el-Nessim

The festival of Sham el-Nessim goes all the way back to the time of the Pharaohs. When families gather in April for this holiday, that is the sign that spring has come again to Egypt. Sham el-Nessim means "sniffing of the breeze." That is exactly what Egyptians do, as they enjoy an outdoor meal in a park or by the banks of the Nile River. Their picnic includes special foods, which they believe prevent disease, such as salt fish, called *fesikh,* and green onions. Children dye eggs many different colors to represent the new life that comes with spring.

Whirling dervishes are famous for their high-paced, spinning dance. The Muslim dancers are actually worshiping **Allah** *as they spin.*

20

This colossus, or huge statue, of Ramses II is so big that a person could sit quite comfortably in one of its ears!

Happy birthday, Ramses II!

Twice a year, a festival is held at Aswan, in the south of Egypt, to honor the great Pharaoh, Ramses II. February 21 is his birthday and October 21 is his **coronation**, the day he was crowned king. In Ramses' famous temple, Abu Simbel, four statues sit in a deep, dark room. On these two days, a ray of sun used to shine all the way through the temple and onto the faces of three of the four statues. During Ramses II's time, these were very special days. Then in the 1960s, when the Aswan High Dam was built, Abu Simbel was moved to save it from the rising waters of the Nile. This massive project involved moving 360,000 tonnes (400,000 tons) of stone and positioning the temple at the same angle to the sun. The sun still shines on the statues twice a year, but one day later than before. Now every year on February 22 and October 22, people celebrate Ramses II's birthday and coronation with folk dancing and musical performances at the reconstructed temple.

Children gaze at the huge statues of Ramses II inside Abu Simbel.

Family events

People in Egypt mark all of life's events, from birth to death, with special ceremonies. These ceremonies always involve the family and often the community, too.

The birth blessing

Seven days after a baby is born, there is a ceremony called *sebou* (pronounced "se-bo-oo"), which means "the seventh day." The baby is placed on the floor and the mother carefully steps over her infant seven times. Grains, such as wheat and rice, are sprinkled to the north, south, east, and west. Everyone invited to the *sebou* makes a lot of noise so that when the baby grows up, he or she will not be startled by loud sounds. Then, all the guests enjoy sweets and strong coffee.

Celebrating marriage

In Egypt, marriages are joyful celebrations that join two families, as well as two people. Muslims are usually married at home. The *imam,* or priest, comes to the bride's home and reads verses from the *Qur'an.* After the readings, a marriage **contract** is signed, usually by the groom and the bride's father. Then, the wedding celebrations begin. Some celebrations take place outside, while others take place in a hotel. The bride is brought into the hall, surrounded by dancers, singers, and tambourine players. Trumpets sound, video crews record the event, and hundreds of guests enjoy the party.

Egyptians love and cherish their children.

An entire village joins a traditional wedding procession along the banks of the Nile. The bride is riding to her wedding on the back of a camel, inside a covered canopy.

Funeral farewells

Like everything else in Egypt, a person's death is part of family and community life. Christian funerals are held in the church and the person who died is buried in a plain wooden coffin. When a Muslim dies, family members follow Islamic tradition and wash the body with love and care, and then wrap it in white cloth. After the washing of the body, male relatives and friends lead a procession to the **mosque** or the cemetery, taking turns carrying the body. It is considered a good deed to join the procession, even if you do not know the person who died.

At the mosque or grave, the *imam* recites prayers aloud, friends and family say silent prayers, and the person is buried. On the evening of the burial, some wealthy families block off the street where the person lived and set up a tent for the **mourners**. Sometimes, they also hire a professional *Qur'an* reader, called a *maqri*. For several evenings after the burial, the *Qur'an* is read in the home of the person who died and food is given to the poor.

Two mourners sit among the graves in a Muslim grave yard.

Workers set up an elaborate funeral tent.

(top) Men play a game of soccer after work.

A family enjoys drinks in a Cairo tearoom.

Like children all over the world, Egyptian children love to play games such as hide-and-seek, piggyback, and *seegha,* a game similar to marbles that is played with pebbles. Some of these games have been traced back to the time of ancient Egypt. Here are some pastimes that you will find in Egypt today.

Get that ball!

Egypt is crazy about soccer. When an important match is played in Cairo, almost every seat at the stadium is taken. People crowd around radios and televisions in their homes and in cafés to follow every move and every goal. It is not only adults who love soccer. Children all over the country kick around a ball every chance they get. If they do not have a soccer ball, they make one out of old socks tied together!

Cafés, conversation, and checkers

Although many people in Egypt work hard, they also know how to relax and enjoy themselves. The cities and towns are full of cafés where men gather for long hours to chat, play a game of checkers, and drink a cup of strong coffee or hot tea. They catch up on the latest news or play backgammon, chess, dominoes, or cards. In the evening, some cafés show videos from Egypt, India, or the United States. In Cairo alone, there are 5000 cafés to choose from. People also like to gather around *asiir* or juice stands. Here, they can quench their thirst with a sip of juice made from sugar cane, limes, tangerines, and guavas.

The Game of the Two Kingdoms

When Egypt was divided into two kingdoms, Upper Egypt was known as the white kingdom and Lower Egypt was known as the red kingdom. After the two kingdoms were united, the Pharaoh wore a double crown of both colors. Today, children sometimes play the Game of Two Kingdoms. Seven bricks are stacked in a pile. Children then divide into two teams, the white team for Upper Egypt and the red team for Lower Egypt. Each team takes turns knocking down the pile with a ball. The first team to demolish the pile wins the game.

(left) With their school bags strapped to their bike racks, these friends hop on their bikes.

(below) A couple of boys row their handmade boats down the Nile.

There are millions of children under the age of fifteen in Egypt, and not enough schools or teachers. Often, children have to go to school in two shifts, morning and afternoon. There may be as many as 45 or 50 students in one classroom. All children are supposed to attend school until the end of junior high. Many continue through high school and university, too. Education is free in the public school system, although some parents pay to send their children to private school.

Zaineb goes to school

It is 7:00 a.m. on a Tuesday morning in Cairo. Zaineb, who is eleven years old, and Jabir, her brother who just turned nine, are getting ready for school. Zaineb is already sitting at the table, dipping her bits of *aysh,* or bread, into a plate of *fuul.* She smacks her lips over the last little bit of the bean paste and calls to her brother, "Jabir, are we going to see you today or tomorrow? Did you forget that school starts at 7:45?"

While Jabir munches his breakfast, Zaineb gathers her books for the day's classes. She is in Grade 5 and is studying Arabic, English, history, geography, science, and mathematics. She checks to make sure that she has her homework. *"Mama,* we're leaving now." Zaineb calls to her mother, who comes out into the hall to give each child a quick hug. "Remember to hurry home. Geda is going to make your favorite dish today. I'll be late getting home from work," Mama says. Zaineb is excited. She loves her grandmother and she loves her grandmother's cooking too. Nobody in the whole world makes better *kofta,* or meatballs, than her *geda.*

Zaineb and Jabir's school is only three blocks from their apartment, so they walk back and forth together every morning and afternoon. They are lucky to live that close. Zaineb's best friend, Laila, has to come on the school bus every day. No matter how early the bus starts out, it always gets caught in a traffic jam!

Zaineb walks to school every day wearing her navy blue school uniform.

At 7:45, the school bell rings. All the children salute the flag, sing the national anthem, and do some exercises in the schoolyard. Then, they file into the school. Each of Zaineb's classes lasts 45 minutes. This year, her favorite subject is geography. She likes learning about faraway places and the geography *ostaz,* or teacher, knows a lot of interesting information.

(above) **Zaineb loves basketball, but she rarely has a chance to play because the older students always seem to be on the court.**

In the middle of the morning, there is a recess break. After eating a sandwich, Zaineb plays hopscotch and skipping games with her friends. By 2:30, the day's classes are over, and Zaineb and her friends pour out of the school. When they get home, they will have a late lunch, the biggest meal of the day. On the way home, they run into a group of tourists who are visiting Cairo. Laila, Zaineb, and all their friends love to practice the English they learned at school. "Please, what is your name?" "Where do you come from?" They giggle a little bit as they flock around the visitors.

As they reach home, Zaineb and Jabir see *geda* waiting at the door to greet them. Delicious aromas waft in from the kitchen. Once the meal is over and *baba,* their dad, has returned from praying at the mosque, Zaineb and Jabir spend a bit more time with *geda* and *baba.* Then, it is time for homework. Every night, Zaineb has a lot of assignments to do. If she is lucky, she finishes early enough to watch some television or go for an evening stroll with her family before she goes to bed.

In Egypt, people dress in a mix of traditional ways and modern styles. Some Egyptians wear traditional clothes that keep them cool in the hot climate. Other people wear clothing that follows the rules of their religion. When they are in public, very religious Muslims cover their heads and their bodies from their wrists to their ankles. Some women also wear a veil across their face. This is part of following *hijab,* a code which tells Muslims to act and dress **modestly**.

A man dressed in traditional clothing sits on the blocks of an ancient monument.

Country clothing

A *fellahin* woman who is married usually puts on a black coatdress over her brightly colored house dress when she leaves her home. She does this to be modest in public. She covers her hair with a long scarf and wears all her jewelry. Her parents gave her silver and gold necklaces, bracelets, and anklets when she got married. This jewelry is her wealth, in case her husband dies or divorces her. *Fellahin* men wear loose cotton robes called *galabiyyahs.* Some men also cover their heads with scarfs wound like a *turban.* On colder days, *fellahin* men wear woolen *galabiyyahs* and jackets. Many *fellahin* still wear their traditional clothes after they move to the city.

City style

Many people wear modern clothes, such as pants, shirts, dresses, and jackets. That is especially true for people who work in offices. When they arrive home from work, many men change out of their modern clothes into a comfortable *galabiyyah.* Others relax in blue jeans and running shoes.

Desert dress

Bedouins know how to dress for the heat of the desert. The men keep cool by wearing layers of loose flowing robes. To prevent heat stroke and to protect their face from the hot sun and sand, they wind a cloth, or *koffiiya,* around their head and neck. Bedouin women have their own style of dress. They wear long black dresses. Married women wrap *asabas,* or black head cloths with colored stitches, around their foreheads. Then, they cover their faces with black veils. For special occasions, Bedouin women wear veils that are decorated with shells or shiny coins.

(above) In Egypt, some women wear head scarves, while other choose not to.

(right) On special occasions, Bedouin women wear black robes with intricate stitching and beadwork.

(below) Like many Egyptians, these young men wear modern clothing.

 # Food

Throughout the centuries, as people from different countries settled in Egypt, they added new ingredients and flavors to Egyptian cooking. Egyptian cooks created tasty dishes by changing Greek, Syrian, Turkish, and Lebanese recipes to fit Egyptian tastes. In every village, town, and city, street vendors cook and sell all kinds of food to people passing by. There is always a delicious snack to try!

Bread and beans

Chances are that, if you lived in Egypt, you would eat *fuul* for breakfast. You might even eat it for lunch or dinner, too. *Fuul* is Egypt's national dish. It is made with stewed beans. Oil, lemon, spices, and sometimes tomatoes are added to the beans. Most people eat their *fuul* with bread or *aysh*. Egyptian bread can be hard and flat, or soft with a pocket. You can stuff fillings like vegetables and sauces inside the pocket to make a sandwich. In some villages, all the women bake bread together. That way, they get to catch up on the latest news while they prepare food for their families.

Pigeon apartments and tasty dishes

Fellahin use mud to build tall pigeon houses called **dovecotes**. They raise pigeons, or *hammams*, for their meat. The pigeons are stuffed with rice and then roasted. This dish is a special treat because many Egyptians cannot afford to eat meat very often.

Dip in! Scooping up **fuul** *with* **aysh** *is a good way to mop the plate clean.*

(opposite) A family eats breakfast together.

Halal meat

Chicken, lamb, and beef are popular foods in Egypt. Many Egyptians do not eat pork because their religion, Islam, forbids it. Muslims eat only *halal*, or lawful foods, that are permitted by the *Qur'an*. They also kill and prepare their food according to the instructions in the *Qur'an*. For example, the butcher must call out *Allah's* name when slaughtering an animal.

Mealtimes

In Egypt, the main meal is usually eaten in the middle of the day. Egyptians often have a nap after this meal, especially during the hotter summer months. *Fellahin* usually have vegetables cooked in butter, tomatoes, and rice for their main meal. They eat the lighter evening meal long after the sun goes down. Some Egyptians use knives and forks when they eat, but *fellahin* use traditional methods and scoop up their food with bread instead of a fork.

A woman perches on a ladder to collect pigeons' eggs from a huge dovecote.

*A **halal** butcher prepares meat at an open-air market.*

A recipe for sweet *koshaf*

Here is an Egyptian recipe for a delicious dessert to satisfy your sweet tooth.

1 cup dried prunes
1 cup dried apricots
1 cup dried figs, halved
$1\frac{1}{2}$ cups raisins
1 cup sugar (more if you like it sweeter)
$2\frac{1}{2}$ cups boiling water

Put all the fruit in a container. Sprinkle the sugar over the fruit and pour the boiling water on top. Cover the container. When the fruit cools down, put the container in the refrigerator. *Koshaf* is most delicious when the fruit is left overnight or for several hours before eating.

31

Glossary

ancestor A person from whom one is descended

barren Unable to produce crops or vegetation

capital A city where the government of a state or country is located

civilization A society with a well-established culture that has existed for a long period of time

colony An area controlled by a distant country

conquer To gain control over a land by using force

contract An agreement between two or more people

Copts Christians from the Church of Egypt.

coronation A ceremony to crown a leader

dam A wall built across a river to hold back water

dervish A member of a Muslim group who has taken a vow of poverty and expresses spirituality through dance

dovecote A structure with nesting holes for pigeons

empire A group of countries under one ruler or government

faith Religious belief

fast To stop eating food or certain kinds of food for religious or health reasons

fertile Able to produce abundant crops or vegetation

heritage Customs, objects, and achievements handed down from earlier generations

holy Having special religious importance

hospitality A welcoming and friendly attitude toward visitors

loom A device used to weave strands of thread together to produce cloth

modestly In a manner that does not seek attention

monument A structure built to remember a person or event

mosque A Muslim place of worship

mourner A person showing grief over a death

nomad A person with no fixed home who moves from place to place

oasis An area in a desert where plants grow because there is water. The plural of oasis is oases.

Pharaoh A ruler of ancient Egypt

pilgrimage A religious journey to a special place

prophet A person who is believed to speak on behalf of God

reign A royal ruler's period of time in power

self-discipline The ability to control one's feelings and actions

shantytown A poor area of a city with many makeshift houses or shacks

temple A building used for religious services

tomb A chamber or room for burying the dead

worship To honor or respect a god

Index

Abu Simbel 21
Akhenaton 7
Alexander the Great 7
Alexandria 7
ancient Egypt 6–7
Arab rule 8
Arabs 10
Aswan High Dam 11, 21
Bedouins 10, 16–17, 28
birth 22
British Empire 9
cafés 24, 25
Cairo 14

camels 10
chores 13
Christianity 10
Cleopatra 7
Eid al-Fitr 19
employment 12, 15
family 13
farming 12
fellahin 12–13, 28
Five Pillars of Islam 18
food 26, 27, 30–31
foreign rule 7
funerals 23

fuul 26, 30
halal 31
Hatshepsut 6
homes 12, 14, 16
independence 9
Islam 8, 10, 18–19
King Farouk 9
King Fuad 9
Lower Egypt 6, 25
Mamluk rule 8
moulids 20
Nasser, Gamal Abdel 9
Nubians 11

pigeon 30
Ramadan 18
Ramses II 7, 21
recipe for *koshaf* 31
Roman Empire 7
Sham el-Nessim 20
Siwans 11
soccer 24
Thutmose III 6
Turkish rule 8, 9
Upper Egypt 6, 25
weddings 11, 22

1 2 3 4 5 6 7 8 9 0 Printed in the USA 5 4 3 2 1 0 9

Two Cairo women examine the fashions in a store window.

Two young men catch up on the latest news.

Traffic on the busy streets of Cairo.

Egyptians having afternoon tea on the terrace of the Cairo Marriott Hotel.

The sun sets on another Cairo day.

The MISR Language School in Cairo

You can see a pyramid from the school playground.

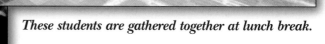

These students are gathered together at lunch break.

It's soccer time!

Perhaps the future leaders of Egypt?

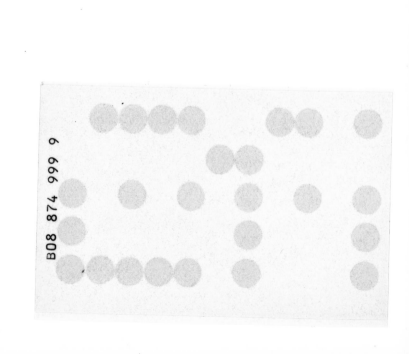

The Lands, Peoples, and Cultures Series

JAPAN: THE LAND

JAPAN: THE PEOPLE

JAPAN: THE CULTURE

CHINA: THE LAND

CHINA: THE PEOPLE

CHINA: THE CULTURE

INDIA: THE LAND

INDIA: THE PEOPLE

INDIA: THE CULTURE

PERU: THE LAND

PERU: THE PEOPLE AND CULTURE

CANADA: THE LAND

CANADA: THE PEOPLE

CANADA: THE CULTURE

CANADA CELEBRATES MULTICULTURALISM

MEXICO: THE LAND

MEXICO: THE PEOPLE

MEXICO: THE CULTURE

TIBET

VIETNAM: THE LAND

VIETNAM: THE PEOPLE

VIETNAM: THE CULTURE

GREECE: THE LAND

GREECE: THE PEOPLE

GREECE: THE CULTURE

ISRAEL: THE LAND

ISRAEL: THE PEOPLE

ISRAEL: THE CULTURE

EGYPT: THE LAND

EGYPT: THE PEOPLE

EGYPT: THE CULTURE

SOUTH AFRICA: THE LAND

SOUTH AFRICA: THE PEOPLE

SOUTH AFRICA: THE CULTURE

RUSSIA: THE LAND

RUSSIA: THE PEOPLE

RUSSIA: THE CULTURE

FRANCE: THE LAND

FRANCE: THE PEOPLE

FRANCE: THE CULTURE

CRABTREE
Publishing Company

U.S.A. $7.95
Canada $9.95
U.K.   £4.50

ISBN 0-86505-313-8

B48 477 994 X

EAN

9 780865 053137

50795>